The Unappreciated Dhurrie

The Unappreciated Dhurrie

A Study of the Traditional
Flatwoven Carpets of India

Text by Steven Cohen

Edited by David Black
and Clive Loveless

David Black Oriental Carpets

We dedicate this book to the prisoners of India's jails
whose work fills its pages.

Figure 11 Dhurrie weavers at a jail in the Bombay Presidency, circa 1907.
From Plate I, Figure 2 of H.J.R Twigg's
"Monograph on the Art and Practice of Carpet Making in the Bombay Presidency".

This book and exhibition were produced by David Black and
Clive Loveless with design by Karen Bowen.
We would particularly like to thank Steven Cohen for his text
and plate captions which were completed with considerable care
and good humour within a tight and often interrupted schedule.
We would also like to thank the following for their help
and hard work:
Peter John Gates and Phillip Paddock for the photography
of the plates.
Gerald Larn for his weave diagrams.
Sir John Thomson, K.C.M.G., British High Commissioner to the
Republic of India and Lady Elizabeth for their encouragement.
Bruce Tozer and Chris Farr for their help "in the wings".
Graham Tanner and C.T.D. Printers Ltd.
The following friends in the trade for their assistance:
Robert Franses, Victor and Graham Franses, Wojtek Grodzinski,
John and Serena Page, Barry Sainsbury, David Salmon,
Leon Sassoon and Vigo Art Gallery Ltd.
David Benardout, Wally Brew, Aminda Correia, Marina Figueira and
Richard Hall for their help in preparing the dhurries for the
exhibition upon which this book is based.

ISBN 0 9505018 5 9

Although antique Indian cotton dhurries have received a great deal of attention from interior decorators over the last ten years they have never been fully appreciated by collectors and enthusiasts of oriental carpets. This book and exhibition are the first serious approach to the subject. Steven Cohen, our author, has given a great deal of time and effort to desk and field research in India and the West. At a time when wishful speculation often replaces true scholarship, as has often been in evidence at the International Oriental Carpet Conferences, it is refreshing and inspiring to work with a sincere scholar who has based his conclusions on hard facts.

It is, of course, extraordinary to realise that most of these dhurries were made by prisoners in Indian jails — people considered by many to be the dregs of society. Yet there is no question that some of these dhurries exhibit superb craftsmanship, sensitive designs and quite delicious colours. There seems to be a paradox here. Or is there, if one considers press reports not so long ago of prisoners in an English jail producing pottery of such a high standard that some dealers convinced themselves they had unearthed a hitherto unknown group of pots made by the famous English potter, Bernard Leach?

We are always amazed and delighted by what comes to light once we begin to prepare an exhibition. The quality of the dhurries that we have discovered has been astonishing. Some are even finer than Sehna Kilims (a type of Persian flatweave often considered the most closely woven of all). Like many people we had always considered dhurries rather lowly creatures. Plate 2 immediately changed that opinion for us. Such incredible work could not possibly exist in isolation. Sure enough, once the search was on other excellent dhurries began to appear.

As with our previous shows the voyage of discovery will not end with the publication of this book and the opening of the exhibition. At the same time, as we have emphasised repeatedly in the past what can be "here today" in seeming profusion can also suddenly be "gone tomorrow". Such may eventually be the case with these beautiful old dhurries.

David Black

LONDON, Spring 1982

5

1

12

14

Figure 1 Large multiple-saph dhurrie from the Deccan.

Figure 12 Prison sample roll.

Figure 14 Detail of 'Noah's Ark' dhurrie.

This exhibition and catalogue are the first devoted entirely to Indian dhurries. Once exposed to a careful selection of these woven masterpieces, the public must wonder how these carpets could have remained unappreciated for so long. They speak for themselves and demand to be recognised as equal to other fine flat-woven carpets. It is hoped than an obvious imbalance will begin to be corrected.

The exhibition of woollen flat-woven carpets at the Textile Museum, Washington, D.C., in 1965 was inspirational, for it encouraged scholars, collectors, dealers and the general public to consider flat-woven carpets in an entirely new perspective. These were now brought in to the mainstream of 'serious' carpet categories and their acceptance and display in major museum collections was assured. The publication of the exhibition catalogue, "From the Bosporus to Samarkand-Flat-Woven Rugs" in 1969, followed by David Black and Clive Loveless's exhibition and publication, "The Undiscovered Kilim" in 1977, were largely responsible for presenting selected examples to the public and allowing them to reach their own conclusions. The attraction was immediate. This exhibition is a logical extension of that process. The criteria and descriptive language used to evaluate flat-woven carpets have been developed and generally accepted and may now be used to describe dhurries. "The Undiscovered Kilim" presented flat-weaves from the Balkans to Southern Iran. "The Unappreciated Dhurrie" will present cotton flat-weaves from the borders of Afghanistan to Bengal.

The early European travellers to the Indian subcontinent were generally unfamiliar with oriental carpets as floorcoverings. The limited supply in Europe was restricted to knotted pile carpets and these were often placed on tables and church altars. When the first English, German and Portuguese adventurers arrived in India, they were able to view flat-woven carpets without preconceptions — and many did appreciate them — but by the end of the nineteenth century the situation had altered.

Sir Thomas Roe:
> ..."Next, I desire yew to provide for mee three or four carpetts of a kynd of cloth stayned and wrought of several sizes and fresh coulors and the best yow can gett at any price. Mr. Terry hath made me in love with them"... April 1, 1617 [1]

Reverend Terry:
> "They make likewise excellent carpets of their cotton wool, in mingled colours, some of them three yards broad and of a great length" 1655 [2]

Mr. Hamilton:
> "The· "dari", a floor covering woven from the cotton of the country, is shown to be an indigenous article... The articles manufactured possess

no artistic merit, and therefore no commercial value for export abroad."
15, March 1907 [3]

These observations were made by educated Englishmen travelling in North-West India. They became aware of the cotton dhurrie and reached opposite conclusions regarding its merit. Is this possible? It is not only possible but quite probable when one considers that dhurries are woven in a tremendous range of qualities, colours, sizes, designs and techniques (each suitable for a specific function) and that one could easily travel or live in India without ever encountering those of the finer quality. It must be assumed that the unfortunate Mr. Hamilton was denied that pleasure!

Sir George Birdwood introduced the dhurrie to the Western world by the publication of his "Industrial Arts of India" in 1880. Unfortunately, he also introduced many misconceptions:

> "Indian carpets are of two kinds, cotton and woollen. Generally they are classed as cotton daris and satrangis, and woollen rugs and carpets, but in fact dari is the native word for a rug, and satrangi for a carpet. Daris and satrangis, however, are perfectly distinct in style and make from the usual Indian pile carpets and rugs. Daris and satrangis are made of cotton and in pattern are usually striped blue and red, or blue and white, or chocolate and blue; and often squares and diamond shapes are introduced, with sometimes gold and silver, producing wild picturesque designs like those seen on the bodice and apron worn by Italian peasant women. They are made chiefly in Bengal and Northern India, and... illustrate the most ancient ornamental designs in India, perhaps earlier even than the migration of the Aryas." [4]

But it was the great Delhi Imperial Exhibition of 1902-3 which really caused the public to notice dhurries for the finest examples from the subcontinent were collected and displayed. Sir George Watt wrote the exhibition catalogue and even devoted four pages and a black and white photograph to Indian dhurries. He largely agreed with Birdwood's evaluation and his pictures of dhurries encouraged people to place orders with Indian prisons to have the most popular designs copied. The fashion for Indian jail dhurries lasted until the 1920's and from that time until the early 1970's not much interest was shown. Gradually, North America and Italian interior decorators re-discovered the simple beauty of these flat-woven carpets and began promoting them under the mistaken title of either "Caucasian" or "Tibetan dhurry carpets"!

What is a Dhurrie?

A dhurrie (also spelled dari, dhurry, and durrie) is an indigenous Indian flat-woven cotton carpet. It is quite often a huge, coarse, thick, striped object and it is this inelegant image which most people (Indian and non-Indian) generally associate with the name. But it can be so much more; and the misconceptions are as numerous as the facts. A distinction between dhurries and satrangis, based on size, is a silly differentiation and really one of language. In North India, "dhurrie" is both Hindustani and Urdu and "satrangi" is Persian. In the South, the identical carpets are called "jamkhani" in Kannada and "jhamakalam" in Tamil. They are made and used by every class, caste, and religious group in India and though perhaps more commonly found in the North, they are certainly popular in the South. The late Dr. Moti Chandra mentioned a list of commercial items inscribed on a copper plate dated 1382 from the South Indian Hindu kingdom of Vijayanagar. They included:

> ... "jambukhana for striped carpets known as jamkhani in Kannada. It is possible that these carpets derived this name from Jamkhandi, a big cloth manufacturing centre in Karnataka." [5]

Statistics on every commercial aspect of Indian life were gathered, analysed and published by Indian civil servants after the turn of the century. These monographs on carpet making have preserved our only accurate reports on the industry; but they have also distorted the record and must be accepted provisionally. The authors and the government were only concerned with goods manufactured for sale. To return to Mr. Latimer's "Monograph on Carpet Making in the Punjab":

> "The industry is of small importance in the Punjab. The trade returns for the province give no separate head for daris, and it is therefore impossible to give any trustworthy estimate of the provincial outturn. It will be seen, however, that it must be of quite inconsiderable extent." [6]

At the time that report was being written there was probably not one village in all of the Punjab where dhurries were not being woven for personal use! If they were not sent to market for sale and the weaver was not a professional "dhurrie weaver" this information would not enter the official reports.

Traditional uses

It was earlier mentioned that the intended use of a dhurrie may determine its design, size, and structure. The most common dhurrie, and the one most likely to be ignored by a foreigner (and forgotten by an Indian) is the bed-size dhurrie. This is usually 2½ – 3½ feet wide and 6-7 feet long. Although most people in India still own and use them, they are rarely seen by non-family members. They are laid directly on the Indian wooden frame bed (charpoy) and other bedding such as mattresses and sheets are laid on top, completely covering the dhurrie. In the morning all is rolled up and put away until the next evening. The bed-size dhurrie is still made by hand in many villages in the Punjab, Haryana, and Uttar Pradesh and in some cases the cotton is still hand spun and naturally dyed. But this has become an exception and power loomed bed dhurries are now easily available.

Another category of dhurrie is one which is used for religious worship. Muslims often pray individually or communally on long narrow cotton dhurries which sometimes reach lengths of thirty-five feet. (See Fig. 1) The pattern usually divides the carpet into individual prayer niches (saphs) with mihrab-shaped arches, hanging lamps, rosettes and other symbols relevant to the religion. The oldest surviving dhurries are probably fragments of Deccani saphs and may date from the early eighteenth century. Hindus may also use very small individual rectangular dhurries called 'asans'. Their purpose is opposite that of a communal carpet; to maintain religious purity and avoid contamination separate seating from their associates is required.

The last category of dhurrie is the room, festival or palace piece. These may assume immense proportions and are among the largest hand woven carpets in the world. They are only limited by the length of material available for loom construction and palace dhurries of $20' \times 60'$ or $25' \times 80'$ are not unknown. Very large dhurries are only made against specific orders but caterers for weddings and storekeepers attached to religious, royal and government institutions generally maintain a supply of large dhurries. Although large, these too are often unobserved. These dhurries, tradition-ally, may lie under a pile carpet in the winter and under an embroidered cloth in the summer. This custom is at least as old as the seventeenth century and can be observed in Mughal miniature paintings. (See Fig. 2)

Prison Dhurries

Students and admirers of textiles usually divide carpets into two major categories. Those hand spun, hand loomed and naturally dyed form a primary and superior group. All those with machine spinning or synthetic dyes fall into a second, inferior group. In the case of Indian dhurries, the division is unacceptable. When dhurries were made in rural areas with hand spun cotton they sometimes achieved a remarkable texture. The superior quality of cotton and the tight, parallel compactness of the fibres produced a texture and lustre similar to fine wool. If the cotton were dyed by a master craftsman the colours could assume a commanding brilliance. And the bold, traditional patterns have the power to inspire respect.

But the finest, most skillfully woven, and most technically sophisticated dhurries are not those of the ancient past but pieces produced between 1880 and 1920 in Indian prisons. The cotton may be either hand spun or machine spun and the dyes are usually a combination of synthetic and natural; but these dhurries are without equal. The fact that they were produced in jails should not be considered derisive. All of the traditional forms of dhurries were woven in jails, i.e. bed size, prayer carpets, room size and huge public size (darbar). Generally they only differed in that a privately produced piece

10

2

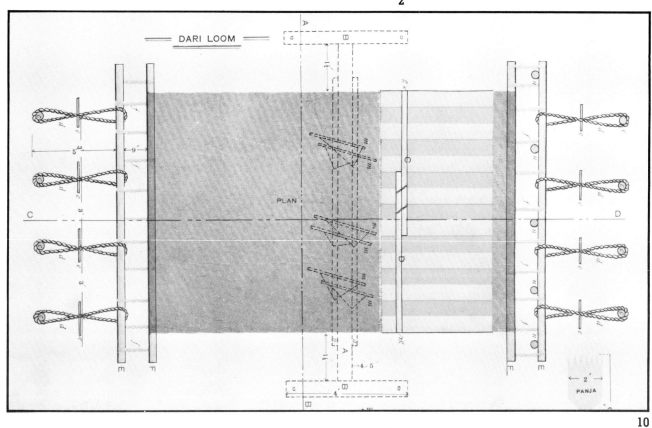

10

Figure 2   Kulu Ragamala Painting circa 1700-1710 (Victoria & Albert Museum i.s. 63-1953)

Figure 10 Dhurrie loom of Delhi Jail, circa 1905. Drawing taken from Latimer's "Carpet Making in the Punjab"

could be of any quality while a jail produced dhurrie had to maintain set standards of construction. The jail did not necessarily need to make a profit and the highest quality pieces could never have been made anywhere but in prison.

Structure

A knowledge of structure is certainly not required in order to be able to appreciate a beautiful carpet. Some feel it to be entirely unimportant. But for those interested in understanding the techniques of dhurrie weaving, the following information has been provided in as simple language as possible. A dhurrie is always weft-faced, that is, the warps are never visible except at the fringes because they are completely covered by the wefts. In its simplest form it is a weft-faced plain tabby weave. (See Fig. 3). In the finer pieces with designs more complicated than simple horizontal stripes, different types of warp and weft sharing techniques are employed. When a weft of one colour meets an opposing weft of another colour the two can share the same warp, one immediately above the other, (See Fig. 4) forming a dovetail joint. This is structurally very strong and is used in the majority of large rural dhurries. When the wefts are tightly packed down before beginning each new row they appear to be continuously level. This technique is suitable for regularly staggered or stepped patterns such as stars, diamonds, crosses and rectangles. Double interlocking (See Fig. 5) is another form of weft and warp sharing but it leaves a slight ridge on one side and the two faces are not completely identical.

The Austrian carpet dealer, Julius Orendi, tried (in his book) to restrict dhurries to dovetailed discontinuous wefts in order to structurally distinguish them from the slit tapestry technique usually found in kilims. He was incorrect. The slit tapestry technique is used in most fine jail dhurries and, in fact, dhurries may employ the entire weaving repertoire of both kilims and European tapestry.

In slit tapestry, a block of one colour is built up independent of the next coloured pattern. When a weft of one colour meets a weft of another colour, in the same row, they turn back on one another without either sharing a common warp or interlocking their wefts. This leaves a gap and is frequently seen when a vertical pattern is woven. (See Fig. 6). The gap limits the design possibilities, to some extent, because if the gap were to continue for too many rows, the fabric would be weak. This can be corrected to some extent by outlining (See Fig. 7) but outlining is usually employed artistically and is time consuming. The slit can also be sewn closed.

Another technique usually reserved for tapestry is eccentric wefting. (See Fig. 8). This is used to form complicated curvilinear patterns and may be part of the Indian tradition or have been introduced through the importation of European tapestry in the sixteenth century. It is even conceivable that imported Egyptian Coptic weaving or Chinese k'o-ssu may have introduced the technique.

The final structural information regards weft floats or weft-float brocading (See Fig. 9). Often the top and bottom six to eight inches of a dhurrie (the striped 'patti') may contain two, three or four rows of weft-float brocading. This is decorative and is produced by a continuous weft which alters its normal tabby weave (one up, one down) by regularly crossing two warps up and two warps down for a limited space. A small raised design is created both front and back and might be reminiscent of the weft-float brocade commonly found on the Baluchi flat-weaves (farasi) of Sind.

Material

The distinctions between dhurries and kilims may be elusive on purely structural grounds but become clearer when discussing material. Generally, dhurries have cotton warps and cotton wefts. Kilims usually have wool warps and wool wefts. But special dhurries in the Deccan and Rajasthan are constructed with cotton warps and silk wefts and some kilims have cotton warps and wool wefts. Both may employ select areas of metal-wrapped silk wefts and the fine Safavid kilims (usually attributed to Kashan) had silk warps, and both plain silk and metal-wrapped silk wefts. To thoroughly confuse the issue, there is a class of Indian flat-weaves called 'druggets' which have a cotton warp and a poor quality wool weft.

The Loom

Dhurries are woven on two basic types of horizontal hand loom; the choice depends on whether the production is rural or professional. Jasleen Dhamija has given an excellent description of the former:

> "The basic technique of weaving a dhurrie in its most primitive form can be seen in the villages of the Punjab and Haryana even today. Here 'durrie' weaving is practiced by the Jat women for their personal use . . . The warp of hand-spun white cotton is prepared by stretching two bamboos secured on the floor by four pegs. The length and the width of the warp are then prepared according to the requirements of the size of the finished 'durrie' by winding it over stretched bamboos. The warp runs parallel to the ground and is six inches above it. Weaving starts at one end with the help of a forked stick, throwing the weft thread across for a single colour going across the entire width of the warp . . . The weaving of the patterned 'durrie' is done with a series of colours depending on the pattern and colours to be used. One colour is woven up to the required width after which it is interlocked with the next colour, and then interlocked again, thus creating a pattern by multiple threads of weft without any extra weft . . ."[7]

13

This simple loom is not suitable for complicated or rapid weaving because there is no mechanism for automatically keeping the shed open and no way of quickly reversing the shed for the next row of wefts. The early monographs contain superb drawings and photographs of jail looms, (See Figures 10 & 11) and for those interested in the more technical aspects of these looms, the information is contained in Captain H.J.R Twigg's "A Monograph on the Art and Practice of Carpet-Making in the Bombay Presidency" and Mr. C. Latimer's "Carpet Making in the Punjab".

Design

The question of design has always been controversial. Sir George Birdwood felt that blue and white striped dhurries were pre-Aryan and he believed that their image was recorded in paintings and sculpture at the Buddhist monuments of Bharut and Ajanta. Perhaps those artifacts existed during Birdwood's lifetime but today they are no longer visible. In fact, striped carpets rarely appear in Indian miniature paintings until the late Sultanate/ early Mughal period; the beginning of the sixteenth century!

When considering designs other than stripes, certain figurative elements such as mosques, minarets, Hindu shrines, votive oil lamps, etc. are definitely religiously derived. But most of the basic geometric figures originate through technical convenience. The most common designs are formed by counting warps and adding or subtracting wefts of one colour in a geometric progression. The staggered "stars", "diamonds", "spearheads", "crosses", "chevrons" and diagonal patterns are all formed that way and have little to do with the figures they supposedly describe. They are simply the easiest figures to weave on a dhurrie loom. This is not to deny that figures have emotional impact and evoke universal responses. They may have originated mechanically; but once invented, they have persisted because of their innate appeal.

Stepped figures are slightly more difficult to weave and it takes more skill to keep the vertical edges sharp. Curvilinear figures are the most difficult to weave and Captain Twigg estimated that only a few prison weavers could ever learn to weave curvilinear figures and that it would take them several years to learn the technique.

The greatest influence on modern dhurries has been European. As Britain gradually took control of India, European designs were introduced and Indians in the cities demanded goods with European patterns. Ghastly Victorian rose blossoms were woven in harsh aniline colours to be followed by bizarre geometric art deco aberrations. Fortunately, those examples have been excluded from the exhibition.

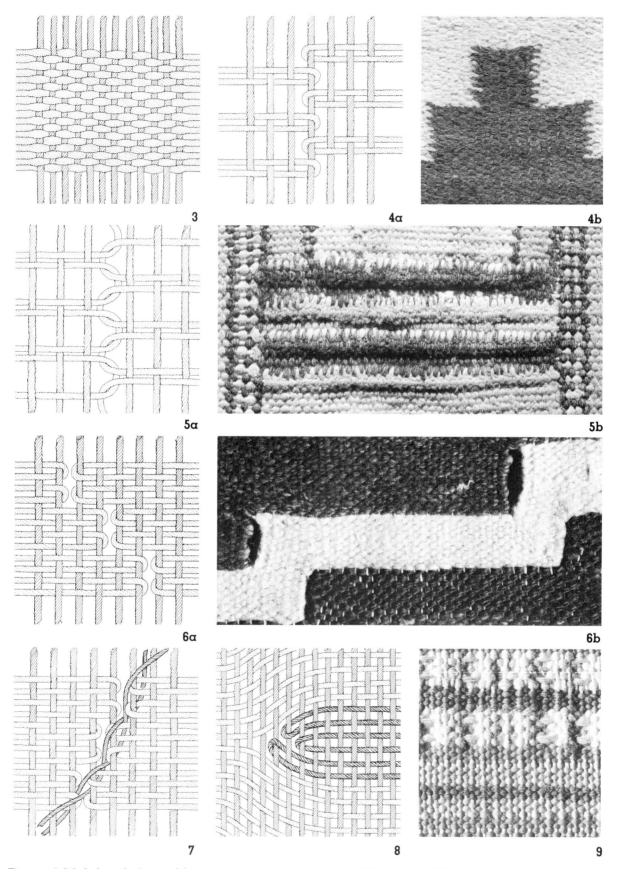

Figure 3 Weft-faced plain tabby weave

Figure 4 a. Dovetailed wefts   b. Dovetailed wefts.

Figure 5 a. Double interlocking.   b. Double interlocking.

Figure 6 a. Slit tapestry. b. Slit tapestry.

Figure 7 Outlining.

Figure 8 Eccentric wefting.

Figure 9 Weft-float brocade.

The rulers of local states such as Bikaner imported pile carpets from Iran, Afghanistan and Chinese Turkistan and these carpets were used as models to weave dhurries. Often even prison officials and their wives were asked to invent designs! Sections of these traditional, imported and invented patterns were eventually woven on long rolls to be used as samples for orders. (See Fig. 12) A border from one design might be paired with a central field from a different design and strange, hybrid dhurries were created. Each jail in an administrative district or Presidency could be sent a similar sample roll; that is why it is impossible, with absolute certainty, to attribute one design to only one jail. For example, Sikarpur jail in Sind developed wonderful designs which travelled to Yaravda jail in Poona when the warden was transferred. When Belgaum jail was built in 1923, the Yaravda jail designs were sent there! The purity of the jail designs does not really exist, but as compensation, the variety of patterns is almost unlimited.

Historical dhurries

When referring to 'historical' textiles, famous private or national collections are usually considered. But with the exception of several late nineteenth and early twentieth century pieces, no important dhurries exist in known collections! The Victoria and Albert Museum did own several dhurries collected when it was still the South Kensington Indian Museum. But most of those were disposed of in the nineteen-fifties. The Indian Museum in Calcutta has many of the dhurries which were displayed in the Delhi Exhibition of 1902-03; but they are neither particularly fine nor interesting (and the exhibit does not appear to have been cleaned since 1904). The Lahore Museum has two dhurries on display but their provenance is uncertain. The Ganga Golden Jubilee Museum in Bikaner has one dhurrie on display (168 BM) which is a pair to Plate No 3 in this exhibition. They were specially woven in the local jail and one (if not both) were housed in the Museum in 1937. The only other dhurrie on display in a museum is in the Bijapur Museum and it, too, was exhibited in the Delhi Exhibition of 1902-03. It created a sensation because it was claimed to have been woven prior to the Mughal Emperor Aurangzeb's conquest of Bijapur in 1628. Upon examination, it does not appear to be earlier than the mid-nineteenth century. It is, however, a faithful copy of a traditional Bijapur multiple-saph dhurrie and represents a continuous link with the past.

There is one dhurrie-like object of extreme importance in the Calico Musuem, Ahmedabad (Accession No. 1423). (See Fig. 13). This was originally from the Amber Palace in Rajasthan and was most likely woven in Lahore circa 1640-50. The warp is of cotton and the weft is wool so it is not a dhurrie from a material point of view. But since it does not use the slit tapestry technique and depends on warp sharing and weft interlocking, it must be considered to be an intermediate step between the local dhurrie tradition and imported kilim influence. Fragments with this design (but with the main border and ground colours reversed) exist, and one with a blue border is in a private collection in London.

For the moment, our knowledge of historical dhurries must depend upon miniature paintings and contemporary descriptions. It is quite easy to find striped carpets in miniatures from circa 1560-1800 but carpets which could be dhurries but display patterns other than stripes are too controversial to be mentioned at this time. Our written evidence is less ambiguous. The official biography of the Emperor Akbar, the "A 'In-i Akbari", circa 1590, says casually:

> "It would take up too much time to describe the jajams, shatrinjis, baluchis and the fine mats which look as if woven of silk."[8]

They are mentioned by John Huyghen Van Linschoten in 1598 and the Italian traveller, Pietro Della Valle, mentioned dhurries frequently during his visit to South India in 1623:

"Letter from Ikkeri contined

> November the seventh. Vitula Sinay Came in the morning to visit our Ambassador at Ikkeri and in his King's name brought with him a Present of Sugar-Canes, Fruits, Sugar and other things to eat, but not any Animal; . . . With the present he sent a piece of Tapestry, not as a Gift, but only for the Ambassador Sig. Gio. Fernandez to make use of in his house. . . ."[9]

"Letter V from Ikkeri Nov. 22, 1623 Continued

> XIV . . . Arrival at the Palace of Venk-tapa Naieka. Then we came to a fourth Gate, guarded with Soldiers, into which only we Franchi, or Christians, and some few others of the Country, were suffe'rd to enter; and we presently found the King, who was seated in a kind of Porch on the opposite side of a small Court, upon a Pavement somewhat rais'd from the Earth, cover'd with a piece of Tapistry something old, and the King sat, after the manners of the East upon a little Quilt on the out-side of the Tent, leaning upon one of the pillars which up-held it on the right hand having at his back two great Cushions of fine white Silk . . ."[10]

> "XV . . . After he had receiv'd and view'd the Present and taken the Iron of the Lance in his hand, which the Ambassador said was of Portugal, they caus'd the rest of us to sit down near the outer wall of the Porch on the left side, upon a rought Carpet, strip'd with white and blew, (of that sort which the Turks and Persians call Kielim) spread upon the pavement of the Porch. . . ."[11]

The Englishman, John Fryer's memoirs contain this lovely description:

> "Letter dated 22 September 1675 from Bombay
> A description of Surat and Journey into Duccan. Letter III Chapter I

At the First entrance into their Houses, Surat Muslims for the greater Respect, they meet at the Portal, and usher Strangers to the place of Entertainment; where, out of common Courtesy, as well as Religion, (when they enter an Holy Place) they pull off their Slippers, and after the usual Salams, seat themselves in Choultries, open to some Tank of purling Water; commonly spread with Carpets, or siturngees, and long round Cushions of Velvet to bolster their Back and Sides, which they use when they ride in their Chariots. . . ."[12]

Conclusion

The eighteenth and early nineteenth centuries saw the gradual but continuous collapse of the Mughal Empire. Internal conflict and the pressures of external colonialism changed Indian society. Political power, wealth and artistic patronage was transferred from decadent Mughal hands to those of the British and their agents. Traditional art forms which had been nurtured and refined for generations were now no longer desired by the new elite. We do not know, for certain, the appearance of the finest court dhurries. None have survived. The Amber Palace kilim/dhurrie may only be an approximation.

While the Court was disintegrating, village life continued almost unchanged. In the villages, simple bed dhurries, prayer carpets, and festival dhurries continued to be woven in traditional forms. Certainly, the 1880's saw the introduction of aniline dyes and machine spun and twisted cotton. These were occasionally used but generally ignored. The local rulers, however, were often wealthy and more easily enticed by the lure of modern "Western" imports. The large palace dhurries of this period begin to display aniline dyes (for unusual colours) and machine spun cotton in the very finest dhurries.

In many instances the transfer of power to the British and their agents, destroyed the finest artistic traditions. The age of classic enamelling, pile carpet weaving, metal inlay, miniature painting and silk brocading had ended. But prison dhurries had no such tradition. They began when enlightened local rulers tried to relieve the monotony of prison life by introducing crafts in their jails. The idea spread to other states and was eventually adopted by the British administered jails. A unique situation was created for the weaver. For a brief period of time, an exhilarating peak of skill was achieved. As in the great Mughal workshops, the weaver was relieved of the necessity to work for a profit. He was inspired by new designs and yet was reinforced by a familiarity with traditional patterns. The result of that rare combination of elements may be seen in this exhibition. Certainly these beautiful carpets must be considered products of a dhurrie renaissance!

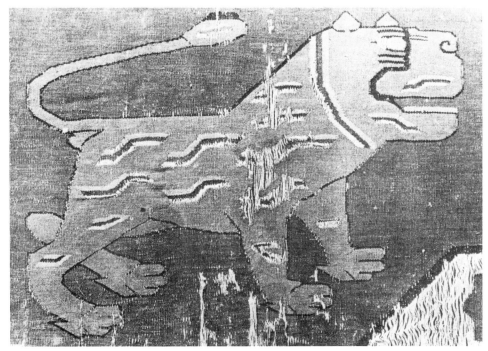

13

Notes

1 Thomas Roe. The Embassy of Sir Thomas Roe to India 1615-1619 As Narrated in his Journal and Correspondence. Edited by William Foster. Oxford University Press. London, 1926. pp. 359-360. Add M.S. 6115 f. 177

2 Ref. Terry. A Voyage to East India. London, 1777.

3 Courtney Latimer. Monograph on Carpet Making in the Punjab 1905-06. Civil and Military Gazette Press. Lahore, 1907. Introductory letter.

4 Sir George Birdwood. Industrial Arts of India. Chapman and Hall Ltd. London, 1880. pp 284-285.

5 Dr. Moti Chandra. Journal of Indian Textile History. Volume VI Ahmedabad, 1961.

6 Courtney Latimer. op. cit. page 2

7 Jasleen Dhamija. Indian Folk Arts and Crafts. National Book Trust. New Delhi, 1970. page 37.

8 Abu 'L-Fazl 'Allami. Translated by H. Blockmann. The A 'In-i Akbari. Volume I. Oriental Reprint Corporation. New Delhi, 1977. page 57.

9 Pietro Della Valle. The Travels of Pietro Della Valla in India. From 1664 translation by G Havers. Hakluyt Society No. 84. London, 1892. Volume II. page 246.

10 Ibid. page 251.

11 Ibid. page 253.

12 John Fryer. A New Account of East India and Persia. Being Nine Year's Travel 1672-1681. Edited by William Crooke, Hakluyt Society Series II Volume XIX. London, 1909. Page 235.

The Author

The Author has studied dhurries in India, Afghanistan, and Pakistan for almost ten years and is currently preparing a doctoral thesis at the School of Oriental and African Studies, London, on "Mughal Floor Coverings".

Figure 13 Mughal Flat-Weave from the Amber Palace (fragment), circa 1640-1650.

1 **Bikaner Bed Dhurrie** circa 1900-1920

This visually stunning, technically superb carpet was woven in the Bikaner central jail. The counterbalance of red and blue effectively frames the central motifs — as does the sophisticated alternation between wide solid stripes (of indigo-blue, red, and pale yellow-green) and the thin curvilinear meanders. The designs are characteristically Rajasthani but show a mixed Hindu-Muslim origin. Flowers and shrubs with long stems, tiny multiple leaves, and large flower heads are traditionally embroidered on Bikaner woollen shawls. But the wine decanters displayed on the centre are part of the Mughal decorative tradition as are the indigo-blue horizontal cypress trees.

The top and bottom of a dhurrie usually consists of several inches of plain coloured stripes called the 'patti'. The 'patti' in this dhurrie is light-blue and red. Next, is an outer border of balanced light-blue and gray 'tooth' pattern; an indigo-blue bar with red meanders flanked by a pair of red, white and indigo-blue weft-float brocading; and a white border decorated by polychrome 'staggered crosses'. Then a red ground border with yellow-green and white 'leaf-and-blossom' meanders followed by a bar of coloured chevrons. Next, a yellow-green bar with red meanders; a white bar with yellow-green meanders; and a final yellow-green inner border decorated with red, white, and indigo-blue 'stars'. Two red bars horizontally encloses the white central ground.

Yellow-green stemmed plants and a diamond terminating in a 'fleur-de-lis' are the main features of the central ground. A dark green elliptical figure encloses two white wine decanters and is surrounded by a gray 'staggered' figure.

Size: 2.31 × 1.35 m or 91 × 51½ inches.
Weave: Weft-faced plain weave, dovetailed wefts, slit tapestry, weft-float brocade.
Warp: Cotton. Z6S. 114 per 100 mm.
Weft: Cotton. Slight Z twist. Approximately 8 – 10 shoots per row. 160 – 164 rows per 100 mm.
Sides: 2 cables; 10 warps each. Z7S.
Colours: 7 White, gray, red, indigo-blue, pale yellow-green, orange, dark green.

Notes on Structural Analysis

Three-figure terms such as Z6S refer to Z: the direction of twist of the individual fibres; 6: the number of individual fibres in a warp; and S, the direction in which all the fibres are twisted together.

Information on sides is limited to the number of cables and the number of warps per cable. Normal dhurries do not have additional material introduced for sides and the ordinary wefts simply carry over one cable, then under the other and reverse direction to begin the next throw of the weft.

2 Bikaner Bed Dhurrie circa 1900-1920

At first glance this dhurrie might appear to be identical to the previous carpet. They were, in fact, copies of slightly different samples; but the subtle differences are well worth examining. The weaver was generally given a sample of one quarter of the design or perhaps a border and a central ground. He was given warp and weft specifications but was allowed to emphasize or minimize a feature by changing its relative size and colour.

The 'stepped-diamond' figures of the previous dhurrie have been replaced by lovely greenish-yellow and pale-blue 16-sided 'stars' (probably borrowed from tile patterns). The greenish-yellow and pale-blue finial of the central ground 'diamond' is less exagerated and now resembles 'Shiva's trident' more than a 'fleur-de-lis'. The pale-green, greenish-yellow and orange stylized 'leaf-and-blossom' meander is limited to horizontal bars which are less technically demanding than continuous horizontal and vertical borders. And the reduction of indigo-blue combined with a substitution of warm orange for red has transformed this very similar dhurrie into something as equally enchanting but quite distinct.

The 'patti' consists of stripes of red, indigo-blue, a mixture of red and orange, pale-blue, and greenish-yellow. There is also weft-float brocading of pale-blue. This is followed by a balanced 'tooth' pattern of pale-blue and greenish-yellow. Stripes (of orange, pale-green, red, and pale-blue) and bars (of pale-green and orange) meet a second outer border of light-beige decorated by polychrome 'staggered crosses'. Then another series of red, pale-green, light-blue, greenish-yellow, and white bars meet the inner orange border which is cheerfully enhanced by 'stars' of greenish-yellow, pale-blue, indigo-blue, and white. Seven bars follow which divide the inner border from the central ground: a thin bar of red and white: a bar of polychrome chevrons; a thin bar of red and greenish-yellow; a wide pale-green bar and an orange meander; a thin bar of red and greenish-yellow; a greenish-yellow bar with 'spearheads'; and a thin red bar.

Size: 2.08 × 1.23 m or 82 × 48½ inches.
Weave: Weft-faced plain weave, dovetailed wefts, slit tapestry, weft-float brocade.
Warp: Cotton. Z6S. 106 per 100 mm.
Weft: Cotton. Slight Z twist. Approximately 8 shoots per row. 156 rows per 100 mm.
Sides: 2 cables; 14 warps each. Z6S.
Colours: 11. Light beige, light gray, pale blue, dark blue, greenish-yellow, pale green, dark green, red, orange, red-yellow mix, white.

3 **Bikaner Bed Dhurrie** circa 1900-1920

This magnificent dhurrie is unique for several reasons. Its companion piece is displayed in the Ganga Golden Jubilee Museum, Bikaner, and it is listed in the museum's catalogue. It was also illustrated in colour in "Bikanir Golden Jubilee 1887-1937", Bombay, 1937.

The design is also unique and a technical tour-de-force. After a simple 'patti' of white and blue all remaining borders are carried completely around the central field. The basic border design is a blossom surrounded by curved leaves, separated from the next set of leaves by a different flower. This is a variation of the 'Herati' border.

In this dhurrie, the first border has simplified the 'leaf-and-blossom' pattern to basic geometric shapes on a red ground. The next border is a balanced 'leaf-and-blossom' meander with polychrome 'diamonds' and 'crosses' separating the leaves. The major border (in rich indigo-blue) is also a variation of the 'leaf-and-blossom' meander. But this is an incredibly complex design; The red, green, and beige leaf meander shades a complex of plant stems, multiple blossoms, buds and tendrils terminating at each corner with a thick white stem. The second beige meander is repeated; then a thin delicate geometric 'pea-flower' meander appears and finally the central ground.

The central ground was probably inspired by a fine Sehna kilim. Maharaja Ganga Singhji of Bikaner was known to have imported old Persian carpets to be used as models in his jail industries and the pale-green, light and dark-blue, white, and beige floral figures vibrate against the rich red ground in a manner too similar to that of a Sehna to be accidental. This Dhurrie is a masterpiece.

Size: 2.285 × 1.9 m or 90 × 75 inches.
Weave: Weft-faced plain weave, dovetailed wefts, slit tapestry with either sewn or single interlocked wefts, outlining.
Warp: Cotton. Z6S. 104 per 100 mm. Each 10 warps knotted at fringe.
Weft: Cotton. Slight Z twist. 6 shoots per row. 172-206 rows per 100 mm.
Sides: 2 cables; 16 warps each. Z6S.
Colours: 7. Red, indigo-blue, light-beige, pale-green, light-blue, white, yellow.

24

4 Uttar Pradesh Bed Dhurrie circa 1900-1920

It is impossible to precisely locate the origin of this dhurrie; but similar pieces were made in Agra, Lucknow and Allahabad. It would be safe to assume that this, too, was woven in a jail in U.P. This is, perhaps, the most colourful, naive dhurrie in the exhibition. The format was probably inspired by European needlepoint but has many elements of Hindu iconography.

The 'patti' is fairly simple: white, green, pink and blue stripes with pink and white weft-floats on blue. Next, a blue outer guard with a pink meander; thin brown and blue stripes; and a white border with highly stylized pink, blue, yellow, and white 'crosses-and-flags'. These 'crosses-and-flags' are residual 'leaves-and-blossoms'. Then a wide pale-beige border of 'diamonds' and 'stars' which, again, was inspired by the 'leaf-and-blossom' motif. The white border is repeated as is the pink meander on blue; and then a series of blue, yellow, and brown cartouches on a white ground.

The central ground is blue with figures of dogs, urns, fish, ducks, men, parrots in cages, a Hindu shrine (with oil lamps, umbrellas, and water pots), trees, flowers, Europeans, mounted soldiers with spears, cannon, and a central 16-sided 'star'.

Size: 2.18 × 1.26 m or 86 × 49½ inches.
Weave: Weft-faced plain weave, dovetailed wefts, slit tapestry, weft-float brocade.
Warp: Cotton. Z6S. 110 per 100 mm. Each 7 warps knotted at fringe.
Weft: Cotton. Slight Z twist. Approximately 6 shoots per row. 188-196 rows per 100 mm.
Sides: 2 cables; 10 warps each, knotted in groups of 5 warps. Z6S.
Colours: 11. Mid-blue, pale-beige, white, bright-pink, bright-green, yellow, black, brown, pale-yellow, green, mid-green.

Preceding page

5 Rajasthani Festival or Palace Dhurrie early 20th century

The large size, sturdy construction, and rich 'abrash' or colour variation indicates that this dhurrie was made for local use. If the simple blue and white 'patti' were ignored, this well balanced design would appear to be tile work. A tiled floor in a country accustomed to packed earth is a great luxury and the immitation of 'tile' patterns is second only to stripes in the dhurrie repertoire.

The outer border is dark indigo-blue with a double row of alternating terra-cotta and white 28-sided 'stepped diamonds'. The central ground is a chequered arrangement of eleven vertical and eleven horizontal rectangles alternating between mid and light-blue. At each conjunction there is a dark indigo-blue 20-sided 'stepped cross'.

Size: 5.77 × 4.83 m or 227 × 190 inches.
Weave: Weft-faced plain weave, dovetailed wefts.
Warp: Cotton. Z10S. 35 per 100 mm.
Weft: Cotton. Slight Z twist. 6 shoots per row. 68-70 rows per 100 mm.
Sides: 2 cables; one cable of 70 warps, one of 60 warps. Hand spun white cotton. Slight Z twist.
Colours: 5. Light-blue, mid-blue, dark indigo-blue, terra-cotta, white.

6 Rajasthani Festival or Palace Dhurrie circa 1900

The simple geometric 'tile' pattern of this dhurrie may seem unsophisticated; but it exhibits a skillful counterbalance between the proportions of the border and the lattice ground. The deep indigo-blue border is framed by a thin white and blue 'patti' on one side and a paler shade of blue on the other. This dark border encloses lighter coloured 28-sided 'stepped crosses'. One cross is pale-yellow with a white interior and the next is white with a pale-yellow interior. The careful play between the colours is maintained in the central ground. The ground is white and is divided by a pale-blue lattice which bisects and crosses pale-blue rectangles. Each alternate rectangle is surrounded by pale-yellow to maintain the same colour balance of pale-yellow, pale-blue, and white in alternating sequences. There is also an exact proportional balance between the size of the border figures and the size of the interior rectangles.

Size: 4.14 × 3.02 m or 163 × 119 inches.
Weave: Weft-faced plain weave, dovetailed wefts.
Warp: Cotton. Z8S. 59 per 100 mm. Originally every 3 warps knotted at fringe.
Weft: Cotton. Slight Z twist. 6 shoots per row. 130 rows per 100 mm.
Sides: New. Pale-blue cotton. 2 cables; one cable of 10 warps and one cable of 8 warps. Z5S. White cotton.
Colours: 4. Pale-blue, indigo-blue, pale-yellow, white.

7 Rajasthani? Festival Dhurrie early 20th century

This 'tile' pattern dhurrie is quite difficult to accurately describe because it is part of a much larger piece and the full dimensions can only be approximated. In colouring and design it is similar to palace pieces from Udaipur.

A white 'patti' meets a thin black guard border framing a row of pale terra-cotta 'diamonds' on a yellow-green ground. The second thin black guard border encloses the central ground which is an 'endless-repeat' white lattice. It encloses pale terra-cotta 'diamonds'. At the lattice intersections, a chocolate 'diamond' contains a yellow-green square.

Size: 1.73 × 3.66 m or 68¼ × 144 inches.
Weave: Weft-faced plain weave, dovetailed wefts, select slit tapestry.
Warp: Cotton: Z4-6S approximately. (No exposed warps). 61 per 100 mm.
Weft: Cotton. Slight Z twist. 3 or 4 shoots per row. 134 rows per 100 mm.
Sides: New. White cotton overcast on all sides.
Colours: 4. White, pale terra-cotta, yellow-green, chocolate.

8 Punjabi Festival Dhurries dated 1901

These colourful dhurries were woven in the Punjab, either in Lahore or Multan jail, and were probably woven for or by Hindus. The stack of small water pots (lota) used during ritual purification appears in each corner. The water pots and flowers are unusual as is the date in the centre. It could have been ordered for a wedding or anniversary celebration or, perhaps, to mark a public memorial for Queen Victoria. Her death was observed with great ceremony all over India.

The treatment of the fringe, i.e. neat twisting, knotting, and braiding is a characteristic of Punjabi dhurries. The 'patti' is white, dark-blue, red, and yellow. A 'key' border of yellow on dark-blue follows. Then a wider border of yellow and orange 'tiles' alternating diagonally and filled with 'staggered diamonds' of dark-blue and white or red and gray-green. The central field is red with polychromatic rows of 'stepped crosses' and 'staggered diamonds' focusing on a central 'stepped diamond' of all the colours.

Size: 4.93 × 2.95 m or 194 × 116 inches.
Weave: Weft-faced plain weave, dovetailed wefts.
Warp: Cotton. Z10S. 40-42 per 100 mm.
Weft: Cotton. Slight Z twist. Approximately 16 shoots per row. 68 rows per 100 mm.
Sides: 2 cables, 20 warps per cable. Z10S.
Colours: 5. Red, gray-green, yellow, dark-blue, white.

34

9 Room Size Dhurrie early 20th century

This fine dhurrie could be considered the standard pattern of dhurrie woven for British officers serving in India. The proportions are meant to fit an officer's quarters or office and the pattern is simple, bold, and masculine. The weave is tight, construction strong, and original cost not prohibitive.

There is a plain white 'patti'; indigo-blue and red guard stripes; red 'key' border on indigo-blue ground; and red, indigo-blue, and red guard stripes framing the central ground. The ground is red with rows of 70-sided 'staggered diamonds'. The outer edge (of the 'diamonds') is indigo-blue, then light-blue, with the same motif echoed in the centre in red. The contrasting colours and fine balance causes the figures to seem to move and the pattern is sometimes referred to as the 'dazzler'.

Size: 3.73 × 2.325 m or 147 × 91½ inches.
Weave: Weft-faced plain weave, dovetailed wefts (possibly 2/2).
Warp: Cotton. Z4S. 49-52 per 100 mm.
Weft: Cotton. Slight Z twist. Approximately 4 shoots per row. 138 rows per 100 mm.
Sides: 2 cables; 10 warps per cable. Z4S.
Colours: 4. Indigo blue, light blue, red, orange.

10 Room Size Dhurries early 20th century

This pair of dhurries is woven in a fairly standard pattern but the quality of the weave is remarkable, and the muted colours combine to elevate these carpets to a select class.

There is a simple 'patti' of white; a dark indigo-blue outer border; dark indigo-blue 'key' on a light-blue ground; another dark indigo-blue guard and then the central field. The field consists of five rows of 44-sided 'stepped diamonds' on a white ground beginning and terminating in rows of 'latch hooks'. There are six groups of these figures and their colours alternate regularly between green, red, dark indigo-blue, light-blue and white.

Size: 2.97 × 1.37 m or 117 × 54 inches.
Weave: Weft-faced plain weave, dovetailed wefts.
Warp: Cotton. Z5S. 60 per 100 mm. Originally each 5 warps knotted at fringe.
Weft: Cotton. Slight Z twist. Approximately 7-8 shoots per row. 196-210 rows per 100 mm.
Sides: 4 cables; each cable 4-7 warps. Z5S.
Colours: 5. Dark indigo-blue, light-blue, white, red, pale-green.

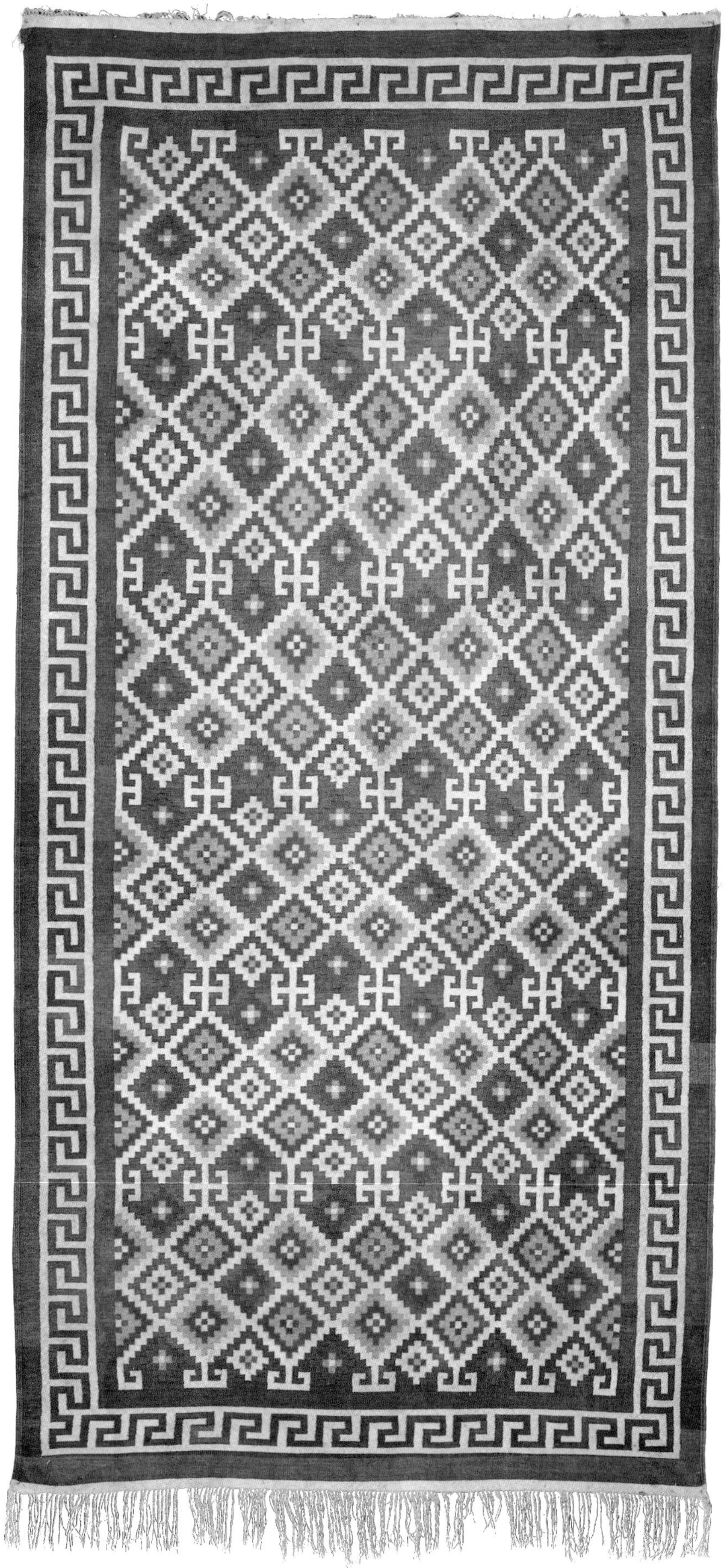

11 Yaravda or Belgaum Bed Dhurrie circa 1910-1930

This pattern was common at Yaravda Central Jail in Poona, and the designs were transferred to Belgaum Central Jail when it was built in 1923.

There is a simple white 'patti'; then a light-red 'key' on a light-blue ground; and a thin purple-black guard stripe. The central ground is pale-cream with a purple-black lattice enclosing a curious variation of the 'staggered cross' or 'diamond'. The horizontal edges of the figures are curved instead of being parallel to the top and bottom and this technique requires considerable skill. The colours of the figures alternate between light-blue with red centres and purple-black with white centres. These produce an overall 'diamond' pattern. At the intersections of the lattice, chequered rectangles of light-red and green are found.

Size: 2.43 × 1.27 m or 96 × 50 inches.
Weave: Weft-faced plain weave, dovetailed wefts, small select slit tapestry (or just 2/2 dovetailing).
Warp: Cotton. Z6S. 84 per 100 mm.
Weft: Cotton. Slight Z twist. Approximately 4 shoots per row. 148 rows per 100 mm.
Colours: 6. Pale cream, light green, light red, light blue, white, faded purple-black.

12 'Bombay Presidency' Room Dhurrie early 20th century

This lovely dhurrie is another example of the many variations possible on a simple theme. The medium-blue ground of both the border and the central ground is divided by 'stepped' terra-cotta and white figures. The border figures are 28-sided with enclosing frames connected to flanking 'stepped latch-hooks'. They alternate between either terra-cotta or white with inner details in the opposite colour. The space created by the meeting of the 'latch-hooks' is filled by terra-cotta half 'stepped-crosses'. In a less abstract form, the central figure and 'latch-hooks' must be considered related to a blossom surrounded by lanceolate leaves — the 'leaf-and-blossom' motif.

The central ground figures are 36-sided 'stepped-diamonds' (of a large format) and smaller 28-sided 'stepped-crosses' which fill the space created by the conjunction of the larger 'diamonds'. The large terra-cotta 'diamonds' are decorated internally by pale-blue or pale-green 'swastiks' (with yellow centres) while the smaller 'crosses' are decorated internally by pale-blue or pale-green 'crosses' (with yellow centres).

Size: 4.48 × 2.825 m or 176 × 111½ inches.
Weave: Weft-faced plain weave, dovetailed wefts (1/1 and 2/2).
Warp: Cotton. Z4S. 55 per 100 mm.
Weft: Cotton. Slight Z twist. 4 shoots per row. 110 rows per 100 mm.
Sides: 2 cables; 8 warps each. Z4S.
Colours: 6. Medium-blue, pale-blue, pale terra-cotta, white, yellow, pale-green.

13 Village Bed Dhurrie circa 1900

This soft, colourful dhurrie has serveral characteristics which indicate a village origin. The cotton is hand-spun and hand-twisted and the weave is fairly loose. The 'patti' is extended and all the design features (except a single enclosing border) are horizontally composed. The 'patti' consists of 34 blue, red, white, black, and yellow stripes; some of which appear to be weft-float brocaded. They are simply multi-coloured single wefts.

An addorsed merlon of black and white frames the central ground. The central ground is a combination of multi-coloured solid stripes alternating between more complex stripes of 'stepped diagonals', 'staggered stars' and 'spearheads' employing the same colours as the 'patti'

Size: 2.08 × 1.08 m or 81½ × 42½ inches.
Weave: Weft-faced plain weave, dovetailed wefts.
Warp: Cotton. Z6S. 34 per 100 mm.
Weft: Cotton. Slight Z twist. 4 shoots per row. 96 rows per 100 mm.
Sides: New. Beige cotton, 2 cables; 8 warps each. Z5S.
Colours: 6. Pale-indigo, terra-cotta, white, yellow, pale-green, black.

14 Bed Dhurrie 'Agra'? circa 1900

This design and colour combination has generally been attributed to Agra. But, in fact, was produced almost everywhere in India. The very tight construction makes it most probable that this was woven in a jail.

A plain white, blue, and white 'patti' is followed by white bars of various widths. The wider bars are decorated with three 'staggered diamonds' in indigo-blue while the narrow bars remain plain.

Size: 1.9 × 1.08 m or 75 × 42½ inches.
Weave: Weft-faced plain weave, dovetailed wefts (1/1 and 2/2).
Warp: Cotton. Z10S. 47-52 per 100 mm.
Weft: Cotton. Slight Z twist. 10 shoots per row. 196-210 rows per 100 mm.
Sides: New. Gray cotton. 2 cables; 6 warps each. Z8S.
Colours: 2. Indigo-blue, white.

15 **Prayer Dhurrie** early 20th century

This individual prayer niche was woven as part of a longer dhurrie to save the time and added cost of individually warping each section. After completion of the entire carpet, either individual saphs or larger multiple sections could be removed. The designs of a stylized prayer niche (mihrab), a finial, and minarets were woven horizontally to speed construction but are viewed vertically.

The 'patti' consists of stripes of light-blue, pink, and indigo-blue with a row of white 'staggered diamonds' on each wide indigo-blue stripe. A white mihrab, minarets, and a finial appear on an indigo-blue ground along with white 'staggered stars' and pink and white 'spearheads'.

Analysis unavailable at time of printing.

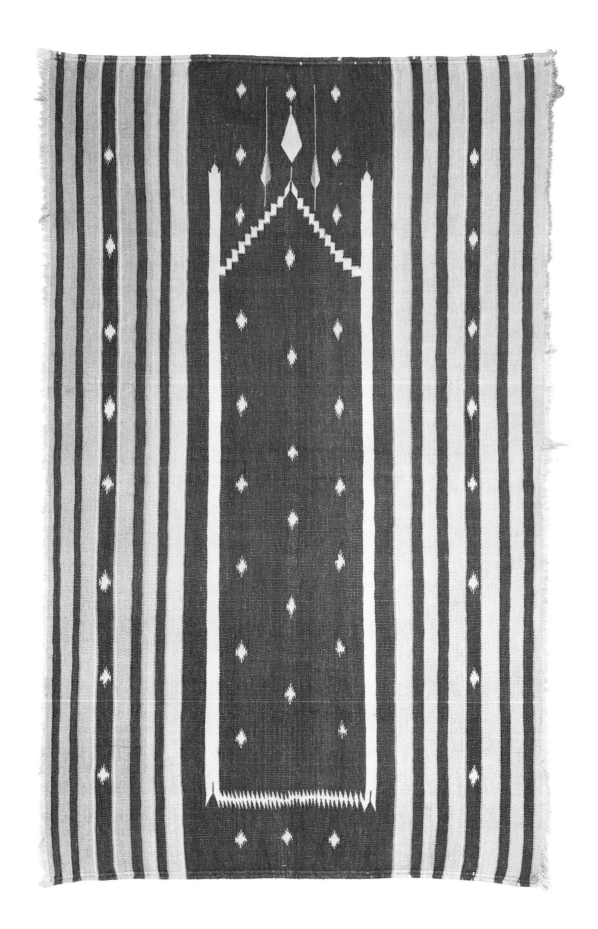

16 Bed Dhurrie early 20th century

The surface simplicity of this bold pattern hides a well conceived design. Wide coloured stripes with stepped ends are placed on an indigo-blue ground. Each wide stripe is divided in two by a narrow bar and the indigo-blue ground separating the coloured stripes is also bisected by a narrow bar. The width of the stripe and the width of the indigo-blue ground is identical. Within each coloured stripe are details of 'staggered diamonds' and 'spearheads' in contrasting colours of light-blue, indigo-blue, terra-cotta and pale-yellow. The entire dhurrie is well balanced and vibrant.

Size: 2.14 × 1.19 m or 84½ × 47 inches.
Weave: Weft-faced plain weave, dovetailed wefts, (1/1 and 2/2).
Warp: Cotton. Z5S. 57 per 100 mm. Each 6 warps knotted at fringe.
Weft: Cotton. Slight Z twist. 6-7 shoots per row. 108 rows per 100 mm.
Sides: 2 Cables; 12 warps each. Z5S.
Colours: 5. Indigo-blue, light-blue, terra-cotta, pale-yellow, white.

17 **Prayer or Room Dhurrie** early 20th century

This design could have been used equally well in a home, a public building, or a mosque. An indigo-blue ground has been divided symetrically by white bars capped with small domes and finials. Each wide bar is flanked by narrower ones and this could be thought of as representing a mosque and two minarets or as a non-symbolic decoration. Small 'staggered diamonds'; half red and blue or half red and white bisect both the wide white bar and the blue ground.

Size: 4.42 × 2.87 m or 174 × 113 inches.
Weave: Weft-faced plain weave, dovetailed wefts.
Warp: Cotton. Z4S. 59 per 100 mm.
Weft: Cotton. Slight Z twist. 3 shoots per row. 104 rows per 100 mm.
Sides: 2 cables; 12 warps per cable. Z4S.
Colours: 3. Indigo-blue, brick-red, white.

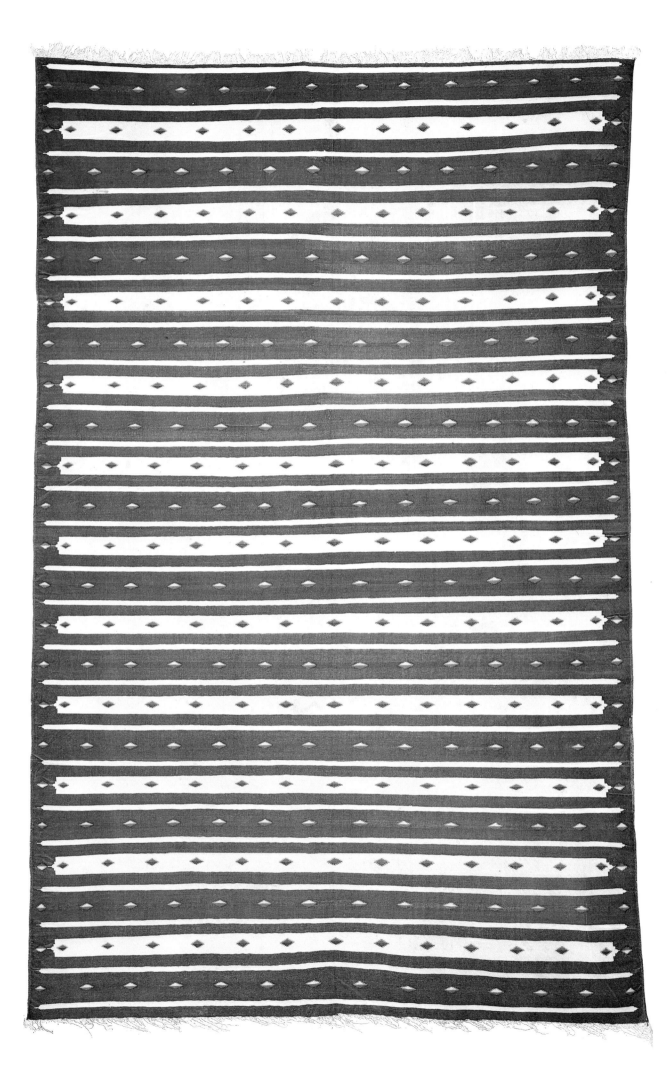

18 Rajasthani Room Dhurrie circa 1900-1920

This refreshing large room dhurrie has many characteristics of the Jaipur and Bikaner pieces. It seems to be relatively new because of its perfect condition and unfaded colours. However, a closer examination reveals a softened cotton fabric which has been produced through much use. This dhurrie has probably been stored for many years.

Two narrow green guard borders decorated with small diamonds flank a white outer border. This outer border has a red meander of 'eight-pointed-stars' with smaller blue 'eight-pointed-stars' filling the gap left by the meander. The pale-blue central ground is horizontally crossed many times by a system of multi-coloured 'garlands'. The string of 'garlands' is a common Indian motif and the colours of these wavy lines are red; blue; red and white; blue and white; pale-beige and red; pale-beige, red and white. As the garlands cross the field horizontally they support a multitude of geometric figures such as 'stars' and 'blossoms'. At various points the garlands rest on Hindu architectural columns. Scattered across the field and unattached to the garlands are isolated 'snowflakes' and 'stepped' eight-armed figures.

The corners are filled with a device which resembles a medieval portcullis and the centre of the dhurrie is dominated by a large eight-armed figure which was probably inspired by a Caucasian central medalion. The four rounded lobes have become 'stepped' and the surrounding leaves have also become 'stepped' and larger, obscuring the original design.

Size: 3.79 × 3.23 m or 149½ × 127 inches.
Weave: Weft-faced plain weave, dovetailed wefts, slit tapestry (either sewn or outlined).
Warp: Cotton. Z4S. 70 per 100 mm (handspun).
Weft: Cotton. Slight Z twist. 7 shoots per row. 106 rows per 100 mm.
Sides: New. Gold cotton. 1 or 2 cables (originally); 4 or 5 warps per cable (originally). Z4S.
Colours: 8. Light-blue, indigo-blue, brick-red, light-green, white, pale-orange, pale-yellow, light beige.

54

19 Room Dhurrie circa 1900

This eccentric dhurrie demonstrates the influence foreign pile carpets played on prison dhurrie design. Obviously, someone possessed or viewed a Yarkand or Tibetan pile carpet and wished to have the design copied on a dhurrie. Although, certainly untraditional in design, the bold pattern and brilliant colours have combined successfully to produce a powerful if somewhat unrefined carpet.

A broad 'patti' of terra-cotta, dull-green and white flanks a wide outer border of indigo-blue. Two narrow guards of white enclose an inner border of terra-cotta. This inner border is decorated with indigo-blue pillars resting on crude dull-green and white 'staggered diamonds' or ellipses and other unidentified figures. The terra-cotta central ground has lovely Chinese-inspired indigo-blue motifs. Corner fretwork seems derived from tendrils and the central medalion is a stylized peony or chrysanthemum.

Size: 2.64 × 1.72 m or 104 × 67½ inches.
Weave: Weft-faced plain weave, dovetailed wefts.
Warp: Cotton. Z4S. 36 per 100 mm. Originally every 2 warps knotted at fringe.
Weft: Cotton. Slight Z twist. 5 shoots per row. 94 rows per 100 mm.
Sides: 2 cables; 22-24 warps per cable. Originally, each 2 warps knotted.
Colours: 4. Indigo-blue, terra-cotta, white, dull green.

56

20 Unique Room Dhurrie circa 1900

This unusual dhurrie is also the result of foreign influence. Normally, a complicated multiple arabesque pattern consisting almost entirely of curvilinear shapes would be considered too difficult to weave. The design is more suited to embroidery and it is almost certain that a Persian or Turkish embroidery was the model.

There is no 'patti'. The entire dhurri is framed in two thin rectangles of dark indigo-blue. A white major border is decorated with an indigo-blue 'leaf-and-blossom' meander and half-blossoms of red and light-blue edge the frame. A fugitive colour once counterbalanced and mirrored the indigo meander, but it has now disappeared. The central ground is cherry-red with two interlaced arabesque systems of leaf, blossom, and tendril in light-blue and pale-cream. Flowers and buds are coloured mid-blue, light-blue, indigo-blue, pale-cream, and the fugitive colour. Stamens are coloured red and orange.

Size: 1.8 × 1.8 m or 71 × 71 inches.
Weave: Weft-faced plain weave, dovetailed wefts, slit tapestry.
Warp: Cotton. Z5S. 80 per 100 mm.
Weft: Cotton. Slight Z twist. 4 shoots per row. 136 rows per 100 mm.
Sides: 2 cables; 10 warps per cable. Z6S.
Colours: 8. Indigo-blue, mid-blue, light-blue, pale-cream, orange, white, cherry-red, fugitive colour.

21 South Indian Room Dhurrie early 20th century

This well used pastel dhurrie was probably placed in the courtyard of a mosque in South India. Although not specifically Muslim oriented, the colour sense and texture is very similar to many multiple-saph prayer dhurries. A pale-pink and indigo-blue 'patti' is decorated with a single blue and white 'staggered diamond' in each of the four corners. This is followed by three borders of equal width. The first is a balanced pale-pink and indigo-blue 'tooth' meander divided by small, connected white 'stepped diamonds'. The second border is composed of alternating pale-blue and white rectangles decorated with pale-pink and white 'staggered spearheads' (on the pale-blue rectangles) and pale-blue 'staggered spearheads' (on the white rectangles). The third border is the same as the first.

The central ground is covered by narrow bands of pale-blue and pale-pink diagonal lines separated by small white 'stepped-crosses'. The next narrow band repeats the same diagonal pattern but faces the opposite direction. This creates a type of 'herring-bone' effect but with different colours, i.e. pale-blue and pale-pink adjacent to each other. The general impression is one of harmonious 'zig-zags' in light colours framed by darker indigo-blue borders.

Size: 3.3 × 2.36 m or 130 × 93 inches.
Weave: Weft-faced plain weave, dovetailed wefts.
Warp: Cotton. Z4S. 72-74 per 100 mm.
Weft: Cotton. Slight Z twist. 5 shoots per row. 108-152 rows per 100 mm.
Sides: New. 2 cables; 8 warps each. Dark blue cotton. Z6S.
Colours: 4. Pale-pink, indigo-blue, pale-blue, white.

22 Room or Festival Dhurrie circa 1900

Using only four colours and a bold pattern (with fine detail) a visually stunning carpet has been produced. If the fine detail were removed, the five bands of border (indigo-blue, light-blue, indigo-blue, light-blue, and terra-cotta) would frame the indigo-blue field without much impact. But the fine terra-cotta and white meanders of 'staggered diamonds' highlight the light-blue while the larger lattice (of terra-cotta and light-blue 'staggered diamonds') glows from its indigo-blue ground. The large format of the lattice is balanced by the delicate diagonal lines (of terra-cotta and white) which cross the central field.

Size: 4.24 × 2.3 m or 167 × 90½ inches.
Weave: Weft-faced plain weave, dovetailed wefts.
Warp: Cotton. Z5S. 85 per 100 mm.
Weft: Cotton. Slight Z twist. 5 shoots per row. 132-138 rows per 100 mm.
Sides: New. Blue cotton. 2 cables; 6 warps each. Z8S.
Colours: 4. Indigo-blue, light-blue, terra-cotta, white.

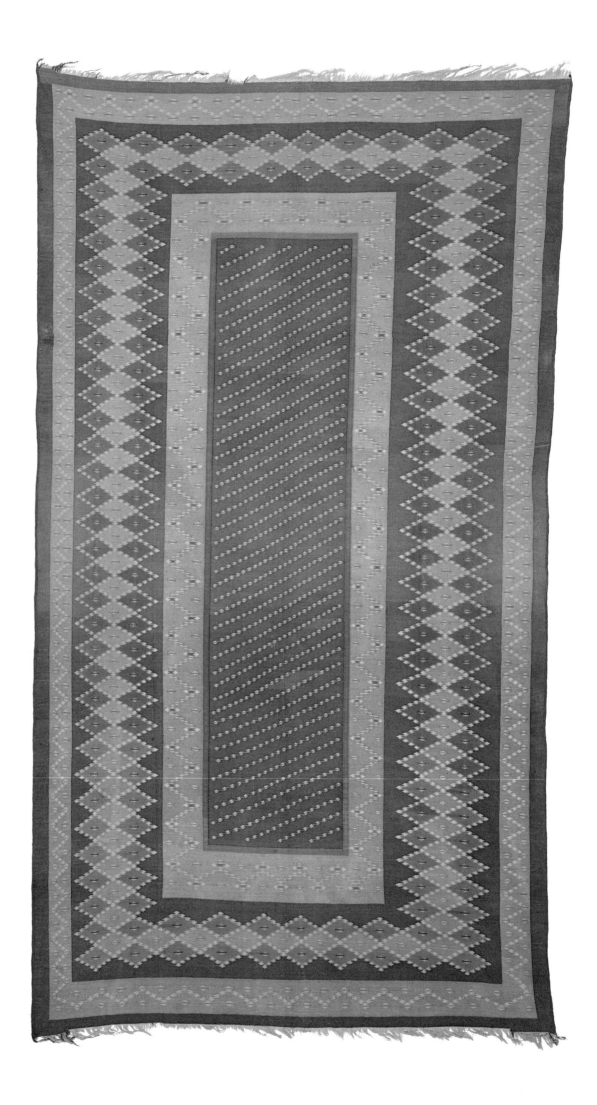

Select Bibliography

F.H. Andrews. Monograph of Carpets. Journal of Indian Art and Industry. Vol. XI. London, 1905-1906.

B.H. Baden-Powell. Handbook of the Manufacturers and Arts of the Punjab. (Volume II of Handbook of the Economic Products of the Punjab). Lahore, 1872.

George C.M. Birdwood. The Industrial Arts of India. South Kensington Museum Art Handbooks. Chapman and Hall Ltd. London, 1880.

David Black and Clive Loveless. The Undiscovered Kilim. London, 1977.

Catalogue and Guide to Ganga Golden Jubilee Museum. Bikaner Department of Archaeology and Museums. Government of Rajasthan. Jaipur, 1961.

A.C. Chatterjee. Notes on the Industries of the United Provinces. Allahabad, 1908.

Dr. Moti Chandra. Costumes and Textiles in the Sultanate Period. Journal of Indian Textile History. Number VI. Ahmedabad, 1961.

Kamaladevi Chattopadhyay. Indian Carpets and Floor Coverings. All India Handicrafts Board. Ministry of Commerce, Government of India. New Delhi. . . .

Kamaladevi Chattopadhyay. Handicrafts of India. Indian Council for Cultural Relations, Indra-prastha Press. New Delhi, 1975.

Jasleen Dhamija. Indian Folk Arts and Crafts. National Book Trust. New Delhi, 1970.

Irene Emery. The Primary Structure of Fabrics. The Textile Museum. Washington D.C., 1980.

Michael Francis and Robert Pinner. "Dhurries, The Traditional Tapestries of India". Hali Magazine No. 3, Vol. 4 March 1982.

Harjeet Singh Gill. Folk Art of the Punjab. Institute of Punjabi Culture. Munshiram Manaharlal Publishers Pvt, Ltd. New Delhi, 1975.

Henry J. Harris. Monograph on the Carpet Weaving Industry of Southern India. Madras, 1908.

Vallery Justin. Flat-Woven Rugs of the World. Van Nostrand Reinhold Co.. New York, 1980.

Anthony Landreau and W. Pickering. From the Bosporus to Samarkand — Flat-Woven Rugs. The Textile Museum. Washington D.C., 1969.

Courtney Latimer. Carpet Making in the Punjab. Journal of Indian Art and Industry. (Vol. XVII. No. 131 July, 1915) W. Griggs & Sons, Ltd.. London, 1915.

John Huyghen Van Linschoten. The Voyage of John Huyghen Van Linschoten to the East Indies. From the Old English translation of 1598. Hakluyt Society. London, 1885. Edited by Arthur Coke Burnell.

John Loring. Durrie Rugs: New Directions for Collectors. Architectural Digest. May-June, 1976.

Rustam J. Mehta. The Handicrafts and Industrial Arts of India. D.B. Taraporavala Sons & Co. Private Ltd.. Bombay, 1960.

N.G. Muherji. A Monograph on Carpet Making in Bengal. Calcutta, 1907.

J.N. Mukharji. Art Manufactures of India. Calcutta, 1888.

Julius Orendi. Das Gesamtwissen Uber Antike Und Neue Teppiche des Orients. Wien, 1930 (sect. 204 pp 186-189).

K.J. Prasad. Monograph on Carpet Making in the United Provinces. Allahabad, 1907.

Vincent Robinson. Eastern Carpets. Henry Sotheran & Co.. London, 1882.

Yaduendra Sahai. Carpet Weaving at Jaipur Jail: The Early Years. Carpet News. Journal of Carpet Industry. Jaipur. Vol. 4. No. 5. Sept-Oct 1980.

C.A. Silberrad. Monograph on Cotton Fabrics Produced in the North Western Provinces and Oudh. Allahabad, 1898.

H.J.R. Twigg. Monograph on the Art and Practice of Carpet Making in the Bombay Presidency. Bombay, 1907.

Dr. Forbes Watson. The Textile Manufactures and the Costumes of the People of India. London, 1866.